The Consistency Gap

The Consistency Gap

Overcoming Failure by *Consistently* Executing the Business Plan

Mark S. Turner

iUniverse, Inc.
Bloomington

The Consistency Gap
Overcoming Failure by Consistently Executing the Business Plan

iUniverse books may be ordered through booksellers or by contacting:
iUniverse
1663 Liberty Drive
Bloomington, IN 47403
www.iuniverse.com
1-800-Authors (1-800-288-4677)

ISBN: 978-0-5953-3807-8 (pbk)
ISBN: 978-0-5957-8596-4 (ebk)
ISBN: 978-0-5956-7013-0 (hbk)

Printed in the United States of America
iUniverse rev. date: 06/14/11

Con-sis-ten-cy *n* **1:** degree of firmness or resistance to movement **2:** measure of harmony, regularity or steady continuity **3:** harmony of conduct or practice with the plan

Contents

Preface

The true test of success over time in any endeavor is consistency.

We all have our favorite restaurant or hotel and any recommendation we make to others is typically based on the fact that the standards are known to be reliably good. When I am trying to communicate how good my local eatery is, I am more inclined to say, *"I have never had a bad meal there"* rather than *"Last night's meal was great."* I do this because I believe it better conveys why I go there. Simply put, they *always* seem to get it right.

I have successfully operated or overseen more than 20 resorts in Europe and in the US over the past 30 years, some of which being large enough to accommodate over 10,000 guests when fully occupied. I have either developed or inherited very workable and attractive business plans and in every case, the greatest challenge by far has always related to maintaining a level of consistency. It is the key to customer loyalty and can be painfully elusive.

Over time, I have come to realize that any of my failures in achieving consistency really stemmed from only two things. I either did not know about the problem or I did know and, for one of a whole host of reasons, had elected not to rectify it. I have learned that the degree of information I receive about my business, and my level of tolerance for things below par, are the only two things that ultimately control the level of consistency between the plan and its execution.

The Consistency Gap initially spotlights the fact that there is always a gap between planning and execution and goes on to define the two causes of that gap. I have given labels and imagery to these two causes and provided tools to help ensure the gap is successfully bridged every time.

Read this book today, apply its principles to your business starting tomorrow, and you will see results in the weeks and months to come.

Introduction

This book is aimed at individuals who are directly responsible for achieving and maintaining the quality of service or product within their organization. Whether you're the manager of a small company or the CEO of a large public firm, you are likely to be the person setting, or at least maintaining, the standards within the business. This makes you ultimately responsible for execution of the business plan and this book is for you.

This book focuses on the gap between planning and execution. It throws the spotlight not on how well crafted the business plan or philosophy is, not on how well each member of the team is trained in his or her specific role, but on the very real - and sometimes very large - gap between the elements of a good plan and its intended results. I call this the *Consistency Gap*.

The coming chapters will show that there are *two things* that cause this gap which, when corrected, bring consistent results in harmony with the goals and philosophies of your organization.

I will demonstrate that *only* two things are responsible for the repetitive failures in execution that undermine even the best of business plans or mission statements. Furthermore, I will show how these failures can unravel any enterprise reliant on a satisfactory customer experience for survival.

As with all complex things, there are usually layers of systems, policies and procedures between the original business concept and its day-to-day execution. These typically begin with a mission statement and general business philosophy and flow into the application stage. I like to think of a good business plan as the ingredients for an irresistible dessert. The goals and values of the organization make up these ingredients. The execution of the plan is the baking or cooking stage. However, no matter how good the ingredients or how talented the kitchen staff, without a recipe, the chances of things coming out exactly as you expected every time are slim.

Assuming that the plan and execution capabilities – the ingredients and cooking method – are fundamentally sound, reliably good end-user experience will come from a consistent application of the recipe by adequately trained personnel.

Throughout the entire application process, regardless of how complex your systems and procedures are for ensuring the best possible consumer experience, only two things govern the ability to successfully make the transition from planning to execution across the Consistency Gap on a repetitive basis. That is not to say there are only two aspects to managing quality in business, but simply that *all aspects* of managing quality, or failing to manage quality, can be distilled into the two elements described in the following chapters.

Two key elements

As I identify and describe these two key elements, the hard part will be to accept that the existence of the Consistency Gap is directly attributable to your abilities in only two fundamental areas. When things go wrong, there is a tendency to think of mitigating circumstances and justifications, citing external forces and matters beyond your control. It will become clear however, that despite their validity, such "explanations" still fit into one or both of the two key elements. A moment ago, I referred to them as abilities. I prefer calling them Fuses.

In each of the two key elements, we all have a fuse that is tripped or blown by the flow rate through it. Too small a fuse and it trips very quickly. Too large a fuse and it may not trip soon enough.

To fully understand this imagery and how it applies to the concepts in this book, I would recommend turning to *Appendix A* for a brief summary of fuses and their general purpose.

As I elaborate on what the two fuses are, I will show how they have a direct bearing on everything that does not meet the required standard in your business. I will also identify ways to check your own fuse ratings, how to check the ratings of those who work for you, and how to determine what needs to be adjusted. From there, I will provide tools to make the necessary corrections.

Chapter 1

The Consistency Gap

The purpose of this book is to focus your attention on just two things that will dramatically improve your ability to manage and so reduce, or even eliminate, the Consistency Gap.

The hardest part for any business operator is to recognize that there is a very real gap between planning and execution. Many people to whom I introduce this concept say the same thing:

"Wait a minute; we've always known there is such a gap."

They say that on the occasions where they have experienced a failure in their business, it has in fact usually been as a result of a failure in the execution stage.

They are sure of two things:

First, that the plan is not the problem. The goals and values of their business are strong. The roadmap is clear and the destination is well marked.

Second, the problem clearly lies in the execution. In spite of the roadmap, and all the training given, someone simply did not execute the plan as intended.

Corrective action modeled on these two beliefs swings the spotlight away from management's responsibilities in this process and fosters a recovery methodology based on "Who messed up, and how do we fix it?" If a good plan and knowing how to execute it were the only things required for success, life would be very simple. However, anyone in business knows that once you rely upon the performance of others, management skills become essential for continued and consistent execution of the plan. Whether you rely on employees, contractors or your shipping service, if the plan is not managed and constantly monitored, a gap between planning and execution begins to open and inconsistency develops.

The first step is to come to terms with the fact that the execution stage is actually on the *other side* of this gap. Take a simple task: keeping the new Italian marble floor in the lobby of your hotel spotless at all times.

The Plan:

1. Choose the best materials for one of the most important areas in your establishment and keep it looking like new.

The Execution:

1. Professional installation of the chosen flooring material.

2. Investment in the appropriate cleaning and long term care products to prolong the good looks of your new investment.

3. Training of the necessary staff to apply these products exactly as recommended by the manufacturer.

If the floor in your hotel lobby is not up to snuff, the problem may lie in the plan. It can simply be that you do not attach enough importance to the appearance of your lobby or that the wrong design or materials have been chosen. At this point, you either must revisit the plan or, to the detriment of your business, stick with the one you have. In either case, you have not yet reached the Consistency Gap.

If not in the plan, the problem may lie in the execution. Perhaps it is in the wrong application of the maintenance materials or in the training and time allocated to do the job. In such cases, these execution flaws can be easily identified and fixed with a simple change. As such, they are on the other side of the Consistency Gap.

If you are actually dealing with your problems at this point, you have already overcome the Gap.

You are now dealing with how well your employees are trained, what resources they have, and how much they care about what they are doing. This aspect of business is relatively easy to get your hands around and surprisingly is not the root cause for many failures or shortcomings in day-to-day operations.

The Consistency Gap exists even where planning is comprehensive and complete and everyone actually knows how to do his or her job well. It is a gap bridged by two things which, when absent either individually or together, make it almost impossible to consistently get it right.

But how is this possible? If it's a great plan, which covers all the bases and everyone has the knowledge and resources to get it done, how can there be failures?

The answer is known to everyone in business: Human Intervention.

Human behavior and, in particular, our degree of effort in most relationships is often governed by a simple principle. Much of how we fulfill our given role in a family, relationship, or organization is determined by what we are able to get away with. Whether we're talking about parents, friends, spouses or employees, the same thing is true. The actions and reactions of those to whom we have made some form of commitment provide useful guidelines for how we are expected or permitted to behave. If a particular action on our part goes unchecked, it becomes passively approved and so gets repeated, especially if it makes our life easier.

If there are instances of drifting away from the plan, without consequences, this is often the easier route for others to follow. If anything but a full application of our skills and resources is ever accepted by management, we are tempted to take this easier approach again in the future.

Even the most honest and dedicated employees fall into this trap because their employer has often unwittingly cleared the way in the first place. Therefore, there is no shot to the conscience, no sense of guilt, and no apparent risk in repeating the behavior in the future.

Think for a moment of a particular policy you have established in your business. It can be about something as basic as employee uniforms, or about a complex administrative procedure. Does this policy ever fail? Are there ever circumstances where you find yourself saying, "How can this have happened? This is against our policy." Again, the first port of call – hopefully after fixing the problem – is finding out who failed to comply with procedure.

A simple illustration would be that of name badges.

Most hospitality-based businesses believe that this is a fundamental part of their customer care philosophy. Identify and personalize your staff to the customer. Flag each employee as a member of a team dedicated to providing help whenever needed.

Yet, when I travel, I see a wide range of success with this concept. Not with the quality or appearance of the chosen badge, or whether the department is listed, or if first name or last name is used. These are all operational decisions guided by overall philosophy. The discrepancies I am talking about relate to the consistent application of the policy. We would all like to think that once the edict has been issued, all employees will at all times adhere rigidly to the plan without any further policing of the program. Of course, the reality is often very different.

I have stayed in small family-run hotels where it was impossible to find an employee without his or her name badge correctly displayed, and I have tried. Likewise, I have stayed in large conference center hotels where three in every ten employees seem to have forgotten to wear it that day. This is not a function of business size, as I have also encountered the same thing in reverse.

Employees at both locations are fundamentally the same. The difference is in the attitude of the management, the consistent application of the policy, and a culture that is clearly understood by the employees.

Quite simply, they can either get away with it or they can't.

It matters little that a business spends a fortune on the highest quality name badges, nor that they have a clearly defined policy stipulating that badges must be worn at all times.

What really matters is that a customer never sees an employee without one!

Chapter 2

The "Fuses"

The Consistency Gap is created by a weakness in one or both of only two elements. To crystallize how much a business relies on the effectiveness of these two elements, I like to compare them to fuses. We all have them for characteristics ranging from temper to patience. Too much flow through one particular fuse causes it to trip. This shuts down the owner's capacity to handle any more of the associated emotion or workload.

The Consistency Gap exists, and moreover thrives, when those who maintain the standards within a business have fuses which are improperly rated in two areas:

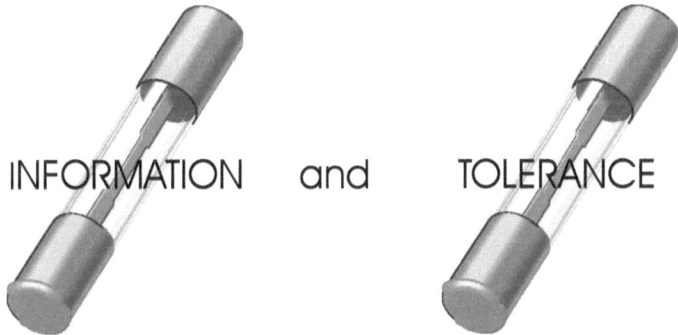

INFORMATION and TOLERANCE

The fuse rating in each case can make the difference between excellence and mediocrity, between consistent service and erratic results.

When we strip away all the tempting excuses, explanations, and attempts at mitigation, one of two circumstances causes uncomfortably frequent occurrences of poor quality or service.

Either those in control who are responsible for application of the plan are simply unaware of the failure, thus it goes uncorrected, or…

They are aware, but tolerant of the results.

Both are hard to fix for different reasons, but a new focus on these two areas can produce spectacular results.

This is the point at which I would invite you to put the theory to the test.

Think of any circumstance that has arisen in your business that you felt did not meet your own expectations or those of your customers. This may be a product with a flaw that slipped through the system or an ongoing failure to maintain the appearance of an area or feature.

What were your thoughts when you became aware of this situation?

"How on earth could I have missed that?"

"Why didn't someone tell me beforehand?"

"I know it's not perfect, but I had no choice."

The point here is that ultimately, the continued existence of the problem *does* come down to one of two things.

A: You either didn't know about the problem.

Or

B: You did but were tolerant of it for any one of a whole host of reasons.

That's it folks! Problems go unresolved and reoccur for one of these two reasons, and none other.

Let me say that one more time: *no other reason*. Whatever you came up with as an unsatisfactory circumstance, ask yourself which of the above applied. Even if you are thinking of some other explanation or justification for why the problem went uncorrected, it still has to be one or the other.

Think for a moment about the opposite being true. In other words:

A: You did know about the problem.

B: You did not tolerate the results.

Can it be that simple? Doesn't "A" plus "B" above mean that the problem would have been successfully addressed? For the most part, yes it does. The real point here is to demonstrate that reversing these two elements does indeed address the problem. It is, of course, necessary to make room for the few occasions when it seems we have no choice but to tolerate the results. I refer to this as the 30/50/20 rule, and I will elaborate on this in Chapter 8.

Once you come to terms with A and B, a basic strategy takes shape which dramatically improves your business practice by tackling these two simple elements. The fewer times you have to say you didn't know about it, and the fewer times you make the decision to tolerate something you should not, the narrower the gap becomes between planning and execution in your business.

More work

Be warned! Every single increase in the rating of your information fuse and every decrease in the rating of your tolerance fuse means more work. Every pause to listen to information and every decision not to tolerate something brings with it additional demands on your time and resources, and new challenges for your determination to get it right at every attempt.

Like many of its kind, this book cannot be read and then placed on a shelf. This will leave you with nothing more than the idea that there is a recipe out there for the ingredients you already have. However, this will not lead to the improvement of the dish. You are being called upon to take some very specific action to check your own fuse ratings. You will be asked to identify if your fuse ratings are high where they should be low or low where they should be high. This means more than an introspective moment or two where the outcome is some self-reassurance that all is well in both areas. It means actually analyzing that which is currently in place within your business. How you act and how you speak - these are the things that tell those who work for you what your fuse ratings are in each case.

When it comes to your information fuse, it is safe to assume that what you don't know about your business *can* hurt you. To keep the Consistency Gap as narrow as possible, your information fuse has to have the highest rating possible.

For tolerance, if you are responsible for setting or maintaining the standards, your degree of tolerance for things not meeting expectations should be zero and this fuse needs to have the lowest rating possible.

As we look at both, you will need to come to terms with the fact that your opinion of your fuse ratings does not matter. What is important is the perception of your ratings by those who work for you. I can't count the times I have heard managers and executives proudly boast that they have an "open door" policy, yet when you speak to their employees, it is pretty clear that nobody dares to knock, or worse yet, go in.

Without realizing it, many managers have slowly but surely created a culture and understanding that while the door may be physically open, frequent traffic over the threshold is certainly not expected and more typically, not welcome. This comes from actions, comments, and nuances that shout in contradiction to any formally announced policy of approachability. These subtle messages override any official policy and are quickly registered in the minds of even the most dedicated employees.

A good place to start in this process is to ask someone who is close to you to rate your information and tolerance fuses. If your business culture is on the cutting edge, you may even make use of reverse appraisals. The most effective way to do this is the select two or three key personnel, not typically reviewed by you personally, and subject yourself to their appraisal of you.

When done properly, with a serious approach by all parties concerned, it can be quite an eye opener for the manager receiving the review. In most cases, their own perceptions are way off the mark compared to how they are viewed within the organization. An untainted exit interview is also a very effective way to garner this information, but in most circumstances this is too late to do any good with the employee being lost.

Chapter 3

INFORMATION: What You Don't Know Can Hurt You

Some of the best business owners and operators I know have a very clear philosophy on information. "Bring it on!"

While the strategy of "plausible deniability" is the bedrock of government administrations worldwide, there is ultimately nothing good that can come from this approach in a business environment. In fact, at the start of the new millennium, business leaders in companies such as Enron, Bear Stearns and Lehman Brothers received pointed reminders from their shareholders, the government and the public at large, that the expectation was for consummate knowledge of what is going on within their organizations.

Let's just pause for a moment and consider the implications of those words.

"Consummate knowledge"

Many of us have a hard time just keeping up with the big stuff, let alone the minutiae. But there is a reason why such a thing is expected and demanded by the many constituents of a business. The judicial system's position is pretty clear. How can you protect yourself, protect your employees, uphold the law, and fulfill all of your fiduciary obligations if you don't know what's going on? Shareholders tend to hold a somewhat unforgiving view on the matter, and the customer simply expects the person in charge to be nothing short of the Oracle.

External expectations aside, there is no better way to secure peace of mind than to be confident that you are always fully informed. Watch your local news or CNN, and pay particular attention to individuals being interviewed on the spot as a result of some regrettable incident. You may well have been in their shoes in the past or at least imagined yourself there, confidently firing back answers to probing and awkward questions. The most impressive among them are those who clearly have all the facts immediately at hand. They have not been blindsided by events. They know what happened, who was involved and, more than likely, what they are already doing about it.

The interviewee has control of the story. He or she is able to limit it to the situation at hand, denying the reporter any license to drift into the more juicy realms of:

"Breaking news – President & CEO knew nothing prior to events unfolding."

In late April of 2004, photographs of prisoner abuse at the Abu Ghraib Prison in Iraq began to reach the media. In a matter of hours, allegations of shocking behavior by British and US military personnel were exposed to the world and a political firestorm soon followed. When George W. Bush, President of the United States, was forced to address the unfolding events, he was called upon to answer questions about the actions taken in connection with the matter by his Secretary of Defense, Donald Rumsfeld.

President Bush was quick to stand behind Secretary Rumsfeld, but the President did confirm that upon news of the abuse reaching the Oval Office, he immediately met with Secretary Rumsfeld to discuss the matter.

It is noteworthy that from this meeting between the Commander in Chief of the US Armed Forces and the second in that chain of command, there was only one thing that the President felt compelled to share with the public about what was said. This was not related to the actual alleged events. It was related to the fact that he should have been told about the existence of the photographs.

The media storm that followed the publication of the photographs soon grew two heads. The outrage toward US Military personnel treating prisoners as depicted in the photographs was to be expected. Competing on an equal footing for news was the story about who knew that the abuse was going on and who didn't. Who had been in possession of this information, for how long and why it was not passed up the chain of command? The President and his Administration spent more time in the early weeks answering questions about the possession of information surrounding the events than about the events themselves.

One could argue that if the right person had known about the behavior and, moreover, the practice of photographing it the story may have broken very differently or perhaps not at all.

Let's go back to the first of the two circumstances to which I attribute many Consistency Gap failures:

The person in control and responsible for application of the plan is not aware of a failure or its causes and it goes uncorrected.

Regardless of how committed you are as a manager, if you don't know about it, your chances to exert any influence on the matter are slim to none.

If something is not as it should be in your business, it is critical that you have that information. It is vital that your entire organization knows that you expect to be provided with such information. In fact, they should know that you demand it.

The possession of such data creates an opportunity for you to manage, to make a decision and take appropriate action. It may be as benign as letting it go in one ear and out the other if your judgment dictates no action is required. On the other hand, it may be an issue crucial to the life of your business and some very serious decisions must be made immediately.

However, if you don't get the information in the first place, you are denied the opportunity to make the necessary decision. Of course, in many cases, it will turn out that the information can be disregarded. But, you must be given the chance to make this evaluation.

I have seen many instances where dedicated employees have been doing their best to communicate something important and useful to their boss.

In the fall of 1989, while playing golf at a large resort on the Algarve in Portugal, I watched the valiant efforts of an employee trying to share information with his supervisor. It seemed pretty important to the employee as he almost leapt on the resort manager coming out of the main hotel entrance. The manager set a brisk pace to his waiting car, while the employee in hot pursuit tried to utter his entire message in the 10 or 12 steps between the hotel entrance and the car door. At the car, our dogged employee did not give up. He saw a chance to continue the explanation through the open driver's window. As the manager nodded his head, the car began to move off down the entrance road.

After a few paces, almost jogging alongside the moving car, our messenger finally saw the futility of the situation and gave up the chase. I got a good look at his face as he turned to walk away and it was abundantly clear he had just learned all he needed to know about how much his boss wanted to hear about the day-to-day operations. As it turned out, he was trying to explain that a truck-load of new golf carts had just been delivered a week early and there was nowhere to put them. The driver of the transporter was apparently ready to drop them on the practice putting green and high tail it back to Lisbon. I finally finished my round of golf and headed back to the clubhouse, and there they were – 20 shiny new golf carts occupying more than half of the green. I have no doubt fellow golfers who did not witness the scene earlier could not understand why on earth they were parked in such an inconvenient location. I am also pretty sure that the resort manager was shocked to see them there upon his return.

At the entrance to the clubhouse were two framed pictures, one of the resident golf professional and the other of the general manager. A beautifully scripted sign spanned the top of both photographs saying, "We very much hope you will enjoy your stay with us. Please do not hesitate to let us know if we can do anything to make it better." From the photograph, the GM seemed like a very approachable guy.

Of course, the problem is time. As with all management duties, there are multiple demands all fighting for a share of the same space in time. On the spot prioritizing squeezes out the minor stuff so we can just get through our day without a meltdown.

However, such prioritizing sends exactly that message. The boss has many more important things to do than listen to his or her employees pass on information all day. Ultimately, the downward spiral sets in. Once you are perceived as having little time to listen, and even less interest, the river of information that should come your way will dry to a trickle in no time at all.

If your message is that you do not expect much in the way of information, that's exactly what you'll get.

In contrast to our golf hotel manager, I have witnessed the busiest executives take the opposite approach. *"Walk with me,"* said a CEO to one of his department heads who was trying to share information at seemingly the worst possible time. *"I am on a pretty tight schedule but if you are able to walk with me I would very much like to hear what you have to say."*

The department head is an acquaintance who shared the tale with me, not because of his boss's willingness to listen to what he had to say, but because of what his boss said in return.

"Thanks for letting me know; I can make good use of that information this afternoon," said the boss.

"But then you already knew that, otherwise why would you chase me down." He went on to say: *"Regardless of how things look, I would like you to always assume I want to hear what you have to say. Force yourself upon me if necessary. I'm still the boss, so I can stop you if this creates a serious problem. My peace of mind comes from assuming you will always do this for me. Thank you!"*

Chapter 4

FUSE TEST # 1: How Is Your Information Fuse?

How do you fare when it comes to your information fuse? Does it trip too quickly? Do you say it is high but your actions say it's low? What can you do to find out?

The first test is to ask what you do to communicate and demonstrate to new and prospective employees that your information fuse has an extremely high rating. This starts with your work colleagues and direct reports. Does everyone who works with and for you have the distinct impression it can't be tripped, no matter how much electrical current – information - flows through it? Do they also know you expect similarly high fuse ratings in them?

Take a moment to identify all the opportunities you have to build and nourish this culture within your business. These can include visual and verbal cues from you, word of mouth, taking full advantage of the initial interview and any official published policy.

> **Visual and verbal cues** - As with most supervisory behavior, how a situation is handled and resolved can provide a blue print for observant employees. Those who are looking to learn about their work environment, and the expectations of the hierarchy, will pick up these messages even in their most subtle and subconscious forms. You may already devote some conscious energy to these

messages, providing cues about how you like things to be done.

You can be sure that good or bad, subconscious or planned, these visual and verbal cues do a great deal to shape the impressions of your existing employees. These employees are the very people you hope will give future prospective employees an enticing run down of what it's like to work for you and your company.

➢ **Word of mouth** - The very existence of the culture is always working for you even when recruiting. Current employees will quickly include, with any word of mouth recommendations, a summary of your expectations. If your existing employees describe you as hard to get to and equally as difficult to engage when reached, this will be the first potential turn off for the kind of employees we all like to hire.

➢ **At the interview** - Assuming that nothing they have heard keeps prospective employees away from the interview table, what are they likely to hear from you or your department heads about the sharing and passing of information in your company?

➢ **Official policy** - Do you have a prepared speech on the subject? What do you say to a prospective employee to let them know that your information fuse cannot be tripped? How do you communicate that failure to share information is both dangerous and limiting to the success of your business? Do you explain not only that you have this expectation, but also, why you have it?

A good start

If the answer to any or all of the above questions is yes, you are off to a good start. However, these are just words - vital words at a crucial time in the hiring process with a very short shelf life.

If you have done your job well at the outset, new employees are going to be looking for tangible evidence of what seemed to be such an important topic at the interview. If they do not begin to see mechanisms, procedures and positive recognition for the sharing of information, the goal is lost. Furthermore, a new and potentially harmful message develops and employees begin to wonder whether you mean what you say and whether you back up your words with action.

There really are people who, when they should be listening, are just waiting for their turn to talk. Most of them do not realize that it is harder than they think to hide this fact. It is a behavior that is all but written across their forehead when they are doing it. This is not a reputation you want for yourself or any member of your management team.

Consider what currently makes up the information-sharing culture within your business. There are four aspects on which you should focus.

1. Look carefully at your own fuse rating.

2. Look at the ratings of your key personnel.

3. Assess the tools and mechanisms currently in place.

4. Review how information sharing is recognized and rewarded.

Once you have taken stock of each aspect, you need to rate each one in a way that is meaningful to you. Using a comparative scoring system or just a suitable adjective in each case, you may draw up a basic chart similar to the one at the end of this chapter. Whatever the method, there is likely to be some "headroom" in all four categories. When completed, you are now on your way to identifying specific targets for improvement.

Let's take a look at each aspect in detail.

1. Your own fuse rating

How do you know if this is high or low? Compared to what or to whom?

No comparisons are necessary, nor are they particularly useful. You simply need to take stock of the culture you have created. If your rating is high, you will already have many of the following mechanisms and procedures in place, sometimes created without realizing it. You will not be able to catch yourself sending any of the contradictory messages previously described.

➢ You will be easy to reach.

➢ You will be easy to talk to when reached.

➢ There will be a clear understanding among your team that any perceived negative consequences of bringing you bad news are far outweighed by the very real consequences of not doing so.

How well do you communicate the latter simple point to every member of your team?

2. The ratings of your key personnel

If you have department heads or supervisors, how well do they echo your own values on this matter?

What do you do to assess and monitor their information fuse ratings?

In all electronic circuits, the highest rated fuse is capable of handling the most flow. However, in the flow of information the ideal situation is to have all fuses in the circuit equal to the one with the highest rating. Assuming this is you, and you should be working under that assumption by now, if the fuses below or before you are weak, the chances for important information reaching you are greatly reduced.

Employees committed to information sharing are soon placed in a very difficult position. They understand the chain of command and that their first obligation is to share all information with their immediate supervisor. If a fuse anywhere in the circuit has a low rating, it will trip long before the flow of information reaches you. Employees are left with an uncomfortable choice. Give up on trying to pass information to their supervisor, or go around them to get to the next person in the reporting chain. Either option is harmful both to the employees and your business.

This is not to say that the function of your key personnel is to simply pass on every scrap of information they receive. Your infrastructure may well delegate some filtering and/or judgment authority to certain members of your team, rather than everyone acting as an unrestricted conduit to you. The important point here is that they get the chance to exercise such filtering or judgment responsibilities in the first place. Employees must be convinced they are expected to share information vertically and horizontally within the organization if blockages are to be avoided. In turn, your key personnel must understand they have been assigned filtering responsibilities not to reduce your workload (wrong message) but because you are placing trust in them to make a sound judgment at their level. If this is always framed with the overriding understanding that your door is truly always open, the culture begins to take root.

That being the goal, how can you assess the information fuse ratings of your key personnel? Are they low? Are they improving?

The first indicators can be found in the discussions that make up the typical Post Mortem examination that takes place after things have gone wrong. Whether the analysis takes on the form of a witch-hunt or just an earnest effort to prevent future repetition, take stock of the language used. The type of suggestions and questions can quickly point to a failure in information sharing and the exact location and level of the low-rated fuses. In all cases, you are looking to identify one of two things when the lack of information has caused the problem. Either the flow did not reach the fuse in the first place, or it did but the fuse tripped. It is of course possible that the flow did reach the fuse and it did not trip, but this is more likely to mean that a lack of action is the cause of the problem, not the lack of information. This is a possible scenario but one which relates to tolerance which we will discuss later.

Initial questions directed at the individual you hold accountable for a problem can include:

"How can you possibly not have known this was going on?"

"Why didn't you know about this, Joe?"

"How could this have gotten by you?"

Translation: Someone in possession of useful information did not share it with Joe in order to prevent the problem or worse, their efforts to share the information failed. Either is an indication that the information sharing culture has shallow roots at that level of your organization.

Alternatively, the questions may be more along the following lines;

"Don't you think this would have been useful to me?"

"Why didn't we talk about this?"

"Why am I only hearing this now?

Translation: Joe is clearly someone you rely on to communicate vital information to you and he failed to do so, or you may have over-delegated to him and your assessment of his judgment skills needs tweaking. Be open-minded here. Your own fuse rating may be the answer to why Joe was unable talk to you about it.

3. The tools and mechanisms currently in place

Tools and mechanisms to promote and facilitate information sharing are deposits in the information culture bank. They represent tangible evidence that you mean what you say. They work for you tirelessly in your absence, showing your employees how easy and important it is to share what they know about day-to-day operations.

Perhaps the most radical of these I have seen in recent years is an internal comment card. It was very similar to the card we all see at hotels, restaurants and even hospitals asking how we found the services, a meal or the amenities.

In this case, the comment cards were designed for and directed to employees. "How was your day at work today?" said the top line. "Was there anything you did not get the chance to share with us today?" read the second line. The usual check boxes appeared below with sufficient blank space in which the employee was encouraged to write any additional information. The form ended by stating emphatically that every card makes its way to the top of the organization and is taken very seriously. Can you think of any better or bolder way of providing a mechanism for employees to share information? Can you say any louder that you are serious about promoting this culture?

A quick chat with some of the employees soon told me that while the card was sometimes used for complaints, these were usually limited to building or equipment issues. Employees quickly started to think of their own uses for the cards. It soon doubled as an employee suggestion program and relieved some of the pressure created by having to make personal contact with someone when information had to be passed on. They liked and used the card and when I asked them why, the overwhelming reply was because it *was* taken seriously. In short, "Because it works!"

With today's technology, it is easier than ever to pass on information. CEOs of many large corporations personally record a weekly or monthly message for their employees. This is usually an informal report that employees can access by telephone and listen to at their leisure. It does wonders for reinforcing the culture from the top. It is also a very effective tool for rumor control. Rumors thrive in vacuums and dark corners. They do not fare well under the bright light of such open communication.

There is nothing more rewarding than hearing a discussion in the lunchroom about what the CEO said in his or her message this week, rather than about what the electrician said to the cleaning crew last night.

Acquiring information first hand should not be ignored. Although it requires more time, inspections in person are sometimes the best way to obtain information in its purest form about a particular facility, product or procedure. Many times, you will find that the extra time taken to make a personal inspection is negligible when compared to the time needed to filter through second or third-hand information for salient points.

4. How is information sharing recognized and rewarded?

If the message is hitting home, employees are very aware of the damaging consequences of not sharing information. But what do they know about the positive effects?

What can be done to recognize and even reward a commitment to the culture you are trying to breed? One of the most effective tools is to contrast the positive results of a particular instance of good information sharing with the potential problems that could have occurred if those concerned had neglected to share what they knew.

When a maintenance employee reports that he has driven a nail into a water line in the wall of a fifth floor bathroom, it is tempting to focus solely on fixing the problem and perhaps what the consequences should be for the apparent lack of due diligence on the part of the hammer wielding staff member. The message being sent here is that it does not pay to report such problems. As is all too common, the belief is that the safest thing to do is creep out, keep quiet, and deal with the anonymous aftermath later.

The opportunity presented to spread the word about your information sharing goals under a real set of circumstances is priceless. It is not only important to give recognition to the employee for coming forward. It is important to play out exactly what could have happened if he or she hadn't come forward. Be detailed and spread the word. You won't be discussing anything openly that hasn't already been thoroughly talked about in the halls and bathrooms by the end of the business day. Include potential repair costs as a result of the flooding, loss of productivity, and possible related accidents to highlight the importance of information sharing. Use the real events to stress how any perceived consequences of coming forward pale in comparison to those of the alternative. Additional training can quickly address the future repetition issue.

That's a lot of information!

The concern I hear most about this approach to information sharing relates to quantity. What will happen if the floodgates are opened? There surely has to be some control of the flow otherwise no work will get done.

In reality, this doesn't result in a constant flow of people through your office door. You will quickly find it is not a matter of volume but one of content.

The danger is not in having to handle a thousand unimportant interactions a day. It is in not being involved in the one important interaction that could have serious consequences to your business.

If you build the right culture, you will not be bogged down in minutia. In fact, you will find yourself well informed, up to date and rarely explaining a failure with the words "I didn't even know about it."

So, with all this in mind, take a shot at summarizing your current position below and set real goals for yourself in each element.

To help with making an assessment in each element, I have listed the things you should consider in the following table.

Take mental stock of the results and use them to rate where you currently stand. You can use any rating device that makes sense to you, but I have found that a simple "Poor/Fair/Good/Excellent" approach works well.

Element	Assessment
What is my fuse rating? Think about how well you listen. How much information you expect and how much you actually get. Consider your employees' impressions of your information fuse rating.	
What are the ratings of my key personnel? Look at how well each member of your staff listens and at how often you are blindsided as a team.	
What tools and mechanisms do I have in place? Reflect on the ways in which you make it easy for people to share information in your business and how you formally communicate your policy. Consider what you actually do to encourage information sharing.	
How do I recognize and reward information sharing? Look back on the use of real events to highlight the benefits of information sharing and consider how you make sure that your employees know it is one of the best things they can do for your business and for you.	

There should be no surprises here. If you judge your own information fuse rating to be Fair or Poor, you can be sure that the rest of the list will be the same. It is this trickle-down effect that works against you when your rating is low and works wonders for you when it is high. The ratings of your key personnel will be low because they will mirror yours. The tools and mechanisms in place will be few because it is not an area that receives your attention. There will be little need for recognition and reward programs for information sharing because there won't be much of it going on.

It follows therefore, that a rating improvement on any element anywhere in this chain has a lifting effect on the elements below it.

You will find that it is almost impossible to improve only one element in this chain. Once you focus on any one element and it begins to improve, you will soon find the entire information-sharing culture gaining momentum and taking on a life of its own.

You will then be halfway there. As with all things created, only care and attention keep them alive. Repeat this culture assessment on a regular basis. Test for its presence and vibrancy often. When you gain ground, fight to prevent falling back. It is three times harder to cover the same ground twice. Worse yet, those supporting your efforts the first time soon begin to question whether the exercise is worthwhile the second time around.

Chapter 5

TOLERANCE: "That Will Do".... Won't Do!

Remember – low tolerance for failure is a good thing. Zero tolerance for failure is a great thing. A low fuse rating means that it takes very little in the way of failure to blow your Tolerance fuse.

Consummate knowledge is one thing, but without acting every time on what you know and what you see, the most you can brag about is that nothing goes wrong without you knowing about it first.

If you are the person who sets the pace for all to follow, your level of tolerance for things below par will determine the quality of your service or product.

Whenever you have been "wowed" as a consumer, you can be sure that it was a direct result of the person in charge having an extremely low tolerance for things not being at their very best.

Go into any large superstore in your neighborhood and look up. Try a quick count of the number of lighting fixtures in the ceiling – they are usually fluorescent panels with two, four or sometimes eight bulbs per panel. Multiply the number of fixtures by the number of bulbs in each. How many light bulbs are burning, sometimes 24 hours a day? This can easily amount to more than 1,000 bulbs. Yet, in the best stores it is surprisingly rare to see any burned out. The discipline needed to support the plan - no burned out bulbs, ever - requires zero tolerance for the sight of just such a thing. Not only does it have to be completely unacceptable to the person in charge, but also every employee has to know that this is something that will not be tolerated.

Excused or accepted once, for whatever reason, a message is created that brings with it those wonderful "benefits":

1. Less effort.

2. Less time.

3. Less cost.

Death by a thousand cuts

Once again, it matters little how you define the standard. The perceived standard will come from what you tolerate. Moreover, the standard practiced every day will only rise to a level set by your tolerance. If your tolerance fuse rating is higher than it should be, the frequency of unsatisfactory performance will rise to *and remain* just below the trip point. This will happen for no other reason than it need do nothing more. The amount of work, time, and money needed to bring down the frequency outweighs the need because the fuse isn't tripping.

The approach of "that will do" spells death to the goal of consistently high standards. When whispered only once, its echo is heard again and again whenever similar circumstances arise. It may be said only occasionally and perhaps only for the little things. Nevertheless, the result is death by a thousand cuts.

When the person responsible for keeping up the standard encounters something that is not as it should be, like it or not one of two seeds gets planted depending on his or her tolerance fuse rating. One is the seed of "zero tolerance," the other is "that will do" or its close cousin, "that will do for now."

However, the thing both seeds have in common is that once planted, they grow without further care or attention. Their branches spread throughout the business and their roots undermine or underpin anything superficial that appears to be to the contrary. The good seeds, like flowers, need more work to achieve spectacular results, whereas the bad seeds, like weeds, seem to do just fine despite a complete lack of attention. In fact, plant too many weeds and you may never be able to grow flowers again.

Many years ago, while sitting at an outside table in a café located at a popular tourist attraction, a very strange sight caught my attention. I was compelled to take a quick snapshot. In this photograph, you can see what I saw.

Armed with two cans of organic paint, one producing a slightly darker green spray than the other, the man in the picture was responsible for "coloring in" any blemishes on the otherwise green and evenly mowed lawn areas.

As he walked away, the lawn behind him was once again a consistent green, free of visual imperfections, just as it had been imagined before it was first created. This initial vision is the first of three steps of any good plan and the beginning of a process seen through to completion by those most successful at what they do.

The First Step is:

To see it this way at the planning stage. This is no more than any of us would do when we put together a new plan. A noble vision of perfection based on ideas, concept drawings, proposals, and pro-forma.

The Second Step is:

To hold fast to the vision over time. Not allowing the mental picture of perfection to be diluted by time and difficulties in implementation. In other words, to see it this way, and *only* this way going forward. The vision never deteriorates. The visionary rejects any imagery of the future that is inconsistent with the plan.

The Third Step is:

To take the vision of perfection, preserving its image over time, and then *never accepting* the reality any other way. This step is what separates those who struggle with the Consistency Gap from those who do not allow the gap to open up in the first place.

Step one is in all of us. Step two takes a little more mental discipline and stamina and starts to weed out those not truly committed to excellence. Step three is tough - really tough - and success here is what separates the leaders in any industry from the rest of the pack.

When putting together the plan, it usually includes an assumption of universal satisfaction. In other words, if the goal is to have an unblemished lawn for your visitors, or a maximum response time to customer requests, or simply a full ketchup bottle on every table, the general assumption in your plan is that all of your customers will encounter these standards, and nothing less, every time.

In the grass painting example, the resort planners cling to what can so quickly be forgotten, or at least "de-prioritized." If a blemish exists for one day out of 365, those who visited the property that day take away an impression less than that envisioned in the plan. It is of no comfort to the consumer to express the rarity of the problem. The problem is only rare to those who have multiple experiences to the contrary. In fact, if someone has only called once, or stayed once, or bought once, it is worthless to try and demonstrate the rarity of the problem. For them, it is one for one.

Painting grass green – "*Crazy!*" you say. What must have been the tolerance fuse rating for the person responsible for appearance at this property? As low as it could possibly be, which in this case translated to a total lack of acceptance for anything but the original picture.

A hidden advantage here is the tolerance fuse for the person concerned gets tripped so quickly that they hardly ever get to experience higher currents. The glaringly obvious deficiencies become non-existent because it is clear to the execution team that a lack of tolerance for a small brown patch of grass means that litter, poor maintenance, and shoddy workmanship are not even within the realm of possibility.

Warning: This is where the justification muscle starts to get a workout. Almost as a reaction to a problem, the temptation is to start thinking of reasons why things have to be tolerated. As soon as you take your first steps down this dangerous path, you will quickly move onto generating support data, analysis and finally justification for not taking any action at all.

In some cases, this muscle can grow so strong it becomes dominant and is the first one to be flexed. This is tolerance for poor standards at its highest and worst.

Also like muscles, tolerance has two modes. The muscles that make us breathe and blink are "automatic." They require no thought or deliberate control. They operate in the subconscious. On the other hand, the muscles we use to pick up something heavy are responding to a more conscious action. They are flexed deliberately for a pre-meditated purpose.

Two modes of tolerance

Tolerance resulting from seeing or hearing of a problem, then electing to do nothing about it, involves a deliberative process and is therefore *Conscious Tolerance*. This exists as a result of a natural or evolved high fuse rating in this area.

Tolerance resulting from simply not seeing the problem, even when in full view, is more like a blind spot and is therefore *Subconscious Tolerance*. I have seen many managers walk past a problem, which has existed for months, and they simply no longer see it.

Your first thought may be that subconscious tolerance presents more risk because it is harder to correct. While this may be true, it is conscious tolerance that really does the damage. Blind spots exist for everyone but we see more than we often care to admit. We certainly ignore more of what we see than we ever want to own up to, even to ourselves. Most of what can be avoided or corrected is lurking somewhere on the radar screen. Blips which continue to show up with every sweep of the screen, refusing to fade until something is done to make them go away. The occurrence of blips that are simply not seen is relatively rare, although it could be argued that the busier the screen the more likely it will be that some blips go unnoticed.

Subconscious Tolerance – is there a cure?

Blind spots can be cured. With the appropriate focus and self-discipline, it is possible to press the "refresh" button and take a new look at your surroundings and procedures. I often hear the phrase "stepping back helps to see the big picture", which implies that things can be missed simply because of proximity and familiarity with the environment. While this can work, many are just not able to disconnect themselves from the task at hand. By definition, it is difficult to estrange yourself from the familiarity that can lead to blind spots.

Think of how the English language sounds to someone who does not speak it. Does it sound fast and complex like languages you do not understand? Does it sound sharp and clean like German, guttural like Dutch or soft and flowing like Italian? The point is, if you speak English you will never know. You have to get a perspective on how it sounds from someone who is not familiar with it.

Rather than stepping back, just reach out to someone who is already at a distance and have him or her tell you what he or she observes. This can be done in a business environment by seeking assessments from those not as close to the problem. They may be consultants, colleagues, friends, fellow employees, or even your customers. As long as they are qualified to understand what they are looking at, they are often in a far better position to spot the things you won't believe you've been missing.

Conscious Tolerance – it's all you

Conscious tolerance is where you *and only you* can make the difference. A decision to start reducing the fuse rating for your own tolerance fuse can have spectacular results for your business.

Remember, if you set the standards, your fuse has to be the lowest of the low, the one that trips before all others. A common trait with those who achieve this involves the use of all five senses.

Their fuse is tripped by the slightest offense to any one of their senses. I recall attending a presentation for the Australian Ambassador to the US in downtown Orlando, Florida in the late 1990's. The facilities and catering were outstanding and the evening went without a hitch. I found out later that things came close to not being ready because the event manager was not happy with the quality of the pen placed by the registration book in the arrival area and wanted a more suitable replacement found. He had gone to the trouble of testing the pen for "feel" and determined it to be of inferior quality. It offended his sense of touch - not to mention his sense of propriety. A small thing to change, but upon reflection, it was one of the many that added to the overall experience of the evening, which was exceptional.

Claims of low tolerance for sub par often come from having nothing more than a discipline for visual inspection. Many things look good but you will never know how the food tastes without tasting it, how the music sounds without listening to it, how the product feels without handling it, or how the room smells without focusing on that particular sense for a moment. Be prepared to put all five senses to work all the time.

Chapter 6

FUSE TEST # 2: How Is Your Tolerance Fuse?

As with your information fuse, *your* opinion of the rating of your fuse doesn't matter. Your actions and degree of follow-up establish the true rating.

Unlike information, the rating of your tolerance fuse is there for all to see. Employees, consumers, or colleagues do not need to work to find out your rating, they just need to look around. They will make their own judgment based on the product or service you provide.

If your tolerance for sub par is too high, this can't be hidden. Whether they are patches of dead grass, rules and procedures not being enforced or just poor customer satisfaction ratings, these signs are read, understood, and followed by your employees.

As with your policy on information sharing, take stock of what you do to demonstrate your tolerance fuse rating. For the times I have gone through this process in my life, it really translated into what I was not doing. This usually means coming to terms with the reality that for the most part things went uncorrected because I allowed that to happen.

Make a list

A good way to help with accepting that anything sub par relates to your tolerance for its existence is to start making a list of the things you consider to be below your ideal standard for your business. As it takes shape, it becomes part wish list, part business assessment, and part strategic plan. Regardless of the items, each made the list because you have thus far elected not to correct it and, for any number of reasons, you are tolerating its presence.

For example:

Dave has a small, specialized shipping business and his primary goal is to deliver a minimum of 98% of his packages on time. Over the past 12 months his records show that he is running closer to 85% on time. This would – or should – find its way onto Dave's list. In addition, the light in one letter of the sign on the front of his shipping warehouse has been out for the past eight weeks. This also should be on his list of things below par.

Dave's List

1. On time percentage is below the goal.

2. Warehouse sign say's "Dave's _hipping Co."

The first benefit of this exercise is the low-hanging fruit that comes into view just by putting pen to paper. The things that make you wonder why you haven't taken care of them jump out immediately. In Dave's case, the light being out on the sign probably has nothing to do with cost or logistics. Dave should not waste this opportunity by just rushing out or issuing instructions to fix it. He should reflect for a moment on the fact that it is only on his list because he has been tolerating it and it has not tripped his tolerance fuse. He should ask himself why not. Whatever explanation he comes up with, the end result will be the revelation that it could easily have been taken care of but it had not yet bothered him enough to get it fixed. His tolerance fuse rating was too high.

Next are the higher branches, harder and more costly to reach. This alone might be why something's presence on the list is tolerated. Dave may look at his on-time shipping percentage and quickly identify why it has slipped. It may be that he needs two more vehicles in his fleet or that he has a lot of new drivers who don't yet know their territory. Again, in either case, the item is on the list because Dave has been tolerating the results of an insufficient vehicle fleet or inadequate driver training. There may be a host of valid reasons why both issues are being tolerated, but if Dave is smart, he should also make room for the fact that the reason could be nothing more than too much work being involved if he decides he is no longer going to tolerate the problem.

Tackling any problem should always include an assessment of the risks associated with inaction and the benefits that come with resolution. However, this assessment of balance only comes into play after a decision has been made to visit the problem. In fact, it is often the very thought of this process, and what you might find out, which is responsible for inaction in the first place.

When training management in the hospitality industry, I have encountered the "don't ask" syndrome. This is an embedded habit of not asking the customer about his or her experience and in particular, not encouraging staff to ask. The superficial explanation appears to be because they don't particularly want to know. So why ask? With probing, it becomes clear this is not entirely true.

The more typical reason for not asking is because it is likely to involve having to do something about the answer. Almost every restaurant I know trains its wait staff to ask the clientele about the quality of the food. Less than half also train and empower their staff to do something about it when the answer is not a good one. You can spot the difference by the use of one of two words.

If your waiter or waitress, in response to a complaint about the temperature of your steak or an inability to substitute one item for another, refers to the kitchen staff or management as *"them"* or *"they,"* disassociation is taking place right before your eyes. He or she does not see it as their responsibility and they do not want to pass up the opportunity to let you know that the problem is not of their making.

They have not been trained to be ready for action after asking the question, "How is your steak sir?" Those who have been properly trained take ownership of the problem and are empowered to fix it. They will typically use the words *"we"* or *"I"* when offering explanations or solutions. Put this to the test next time you are dining out. The results are striking.

My position as a consumer is pretty straightforward. If you are not prepared to do anything about it, then don't ask.

The fear of consequences can be all that is needed to promote tolerance for substandard performance. It is worth exploring the reason for such fear. This can be just plain laziness, nothing more than "too much trouble." Most who suffer from this ailment are unlikely to ever read this book.

But it is not always laziness. It can sometimes be a realization that the consequences are too great. The costs involved in rectification are too high. The complexity of the problem may place resolution beyond your skill base or even outside the realm of possibility. To reach these conclusions, at least an analysis has been done.

Do not lose sight of the fact that such conclusions are still decisions on your part to act or not to act, rather than the result of any external influence.

Once you have accepted that most things which you feel to be below par within your business are that way because of a conscious decision on your part, you are well on the way to fixing the things which can be fixed. You are well on the way to promoting a culture of zero tolerance for substandard work or products.

The same focus areas from Chapter Four apply here too. Take a close look at your own fuse rating, the ratings of your key personnel, and the mechanisms you have in place to foster low to zero tolerance.

Once again, the following detail will help guide you through this process.

Your own fuse rating

This one is relatively easy. What do you let people get away with and how often?

Any business will provide an endless flow of current to test your tolerance fuse. The big things are usually so obvious that they trip your fuse immediately and put you in recovery mode. What about the small stuff? This is low voltage current and can easily trickle through your fuse unnoticed. Remember: death by a thousand cuts.

Your tolerance fuse has to be rated in fractions of an amp, sensitive to the lightest current, tripped at the first sign of a problem.

Once again, if your rating is already low, the culture within your organization will reflect this fact. It will be one of "Get it right the first time." Employees and management will know that there is no point presenting something which is below par because this will simply mean having to go back and do it again.

More often than not, those responsible for a particular task or product will know when you are likely to judge it to be below par. The mindset of someone faced with a choice to present a task or product for approval, which they already know to be below par, is typically one of the following depending on what they know, or think they know, about their manager's standards:

"It's worth a try."

OR

"Don't even bother; you're wasting your time."

Which is the predominant attitude within your business? Does every member of your team instinctively know that it is the latter? Once you have cultivated this reputation, the culture is in place and working for you all the time. You will hear employees telling other employees that they are wasting their time producing or submitting anything below standard. Your message clearly repeated for you in your absence time and time again.

Of course, there will be times when you have elected to tolerate something after considering all the facts and the consequences. However, it is vital that you explain when and why you are making this choice. Confusion will soon set in if you are working hard to portray a very low tolerance level for substandard performance yet appearing to let things go from time to time.

More often than not, those who see a conflict between policy and practice do so because they have not been involved in or informed of the process that led to the policy override, and it therefore doesn't seem to make sense. It is easy to fall into the trap of assuming your decision to tolerate something makes sense to others because you know in your mind and heart that it was the right thing to do.

For example, your stated policy and values may say that you will absolutely not accept missing a shipping deadline. However, one day you make a decision to do exactly that because you noticed a flaw in the product that would completely destroy your reputation and relationship with the customer. If you make that decision in a vacuum, without explaining that it was the severity of the consequences that forced you to sell your stated values short, the message can become very confused.

When this is necessary, make it absolutely clear why you elected to tolerate the problem. This is your best chance to communicate just how much is necessary to get you to consider operating below the standard, even for a single instance.

There is a difference between paying out rope as a strategic move and loosening your grip on it completely. The outward appearance for both can be exactly the same and without explanation; employees will tend to assume you are doing the latter.

The more your employees and management know about your thought process in such circumstances, the more they will understand that slacking off on the standards is highly undesirable and an absolute last resort in every case.

The ratings of your key personnel

There is one thing that is common in all electrical circuits. The flow of current is stepped down from the main supply to the point of final use. In the circuit, individual fuse ratings start very high and gradually reduce as the circuit winds its way through the distribution line.

It is a safe assumption that anything reaching the lowest-rated tolerance fuse in the line passed without interruption through every fuse it encountered along the way. This is a good indication that those fuses are at best, rated equal to your own, but are more likely rated higher and therefore indicate a greater degree of tolerance than your own for anything below par.

Business habits and time sensitivities compel us to fix problems as they occur. We rarely take the time needed to find out, in a constructive way, why it got to the top. You can almost guarantee that by the time you see the problem, it has existed long enough for a good number of your customers to have suffered from its effects.

If the zero tolerance culture in your business is healthy, the fuse ratings of all your key personnel are so low that a problem can't survive the passage to the top. For problems that get to you uncorrected, or even unnoticed, you can regard the tolerance circuit in your organization as having failed. Fuse ratings down the line were simply too high to be tripped, allowing the current to flow uninterrupted all the way to the end of the line.

After fixing the problem, take the time to trace the issue back through the circuit one level at a time. At each level, identify why the fuse in question was not tripped. Use the opportunity to find out why specific members of your team had a fuse rating which was too high to catch the problem. Be ready for some uncomfortable revelations. The answer can often be one of inadequate training or poorly communicated standards and ideals. When you have it right, every member of your team understands his or her role within the circuit. They know the function of their own fuse and at what level it should be set.

In the late fall of 1995, I was enjoying a day off at an amusement park in Central Florida. Although this was by no means one of the "big boys," the park seemed very well kept and well organized. After a full morning, I was taking a well-earned rest at one of the food outlets, sitting in the sun and watching the frenzy of activity surrounding an oval shaped flowerbed close to my table.

The staff was removing the flowers and it soon became clear that they were preparing the bed for the arrival of the park's main Christmas tree. Lighting strands and abnormally large tree ornaments were arriving in dozens of boxes and everyone gave the appearance of having performed this task many times before.

One staff member, who appeared to be a lead or supervisor, was assigned to painting the knee high decorative iron fence that enclosed the oval flowerbed. All the appropriate signs were in place and he was busy applying a fresh coat of dark green paint to the fence. My grandfather would have called the color *British Racing Green*. The fence was already painted this color and what struck me most was that the section of the fence not yet painted looked just as good as the freshly painted area.

After 20 minutes of observation, my curiosity got the better of me and I swung my legs over the attached bench of the table at which I was seated to spin around and face the painter. Leaning forward to catch his attention, I complimented him on his fine work. I then felt compelled to point out that the fence was in such good shape, it didn't look to me like it needed re-painting. He turned to face me and politely said:

"With respect sir, if it looked like it needed painting, we would have been too late!"

All kinds of thoughts came to mind. This was not a trained response. This was not something that he had been told to say in the event that a customer should one day ask him why he was painting a fence that appeared to be in perfectly good shape. This was an employee, presumably charged with the appearance of the property, expressing his low tolerance for anything less than perfection. Furthermore, he was clearly operating in an environment where this attitude was encouraged, and he clearly understood his role in not letting things fall below par.

How did he get that way? Granted, he may have been a diligent worker by nature, but many businesses have the unfortunate capacity to purge this kind of attitude from an employee within his or her first few weeks of employment. Such an attitude can only survive when nurtured, promoted and rewarded.

When assessing the tolerance fuse ratings of your management and employees, start with the obvious. What appears to get through their fuse? What is the quality and consistency of their day to day output? Remember - when it comes to the tolerance fuse rating, the indicators are there for the viewing.

But also be ready for some surprises. A low rating may be the result of how the employee sees his or her role based on the original training received. A problem may get by without being resolved because of a lack of empowerment. Incomplete training may leave them ill equipped to address the problem. While these can all be fixed, it is worth making sure that a failsafe has been built into your circuit.

Make it clear that even when an employee consciously tolerates a problem and lets it pass by unresolved, you expect that although his or her tolerance fuse failed to trip, their information fuse should still have acted as a failsafe. The first thought that should cross the mind of an employee facing a problem they do not feel empowered or trained to fix is to quickly tell someone who is.

There can be occasions when an employee knows that what he or she is dealing with is simply not right. In some cases, he or she may not even be sure why – just that it doesn't "feel" right. There is little hope of the employee correcting the problem, as his or her tolerance fuse has not really been tripped. However, all is not lost if they have a good understanding of your information sharing policies and their information fuse has a high enough rating. They will know that they can and should immediately pass their concerns on to someone up the chain of command.

The mechanisms in place to foster low tolerance

What do you currently do to foster an environment of low tolerance for substandard performance?

The first step is to notice!

In business, we are all quick to realize that things go wrong for a reason. We are sure that there is a root cause that needs to be tracked down and eliminated for the future. We tend to be certain of two things:

1. Things rarely go wrong by accident.

2. More often than not, the error is human.

We apply this knowledge every day, and it's clear to any team member that there will be a detailed analysis of a problem whenever one occurs.

What we are not as quick to keep in mind, are two more things:

1. Things rarely go right by accident.

2. More often than not, the cause is human.

Your reaction to a problem is always noted and acted upon, as it should be if you are running the ship. Likewise, your reaction to the absence of problems is also noted.

While running a large resort in the UK in the late 80's, I recall that in the first year, I was constantly annoyed by the fact that the paper hand towel dispensers in many of the public bathrooms were empty as often as they were full. This would drive me crazy and the usual "let's get this fixed" meetings would follow. In the second year, the problem simply went away. From then on, pulling the lever always produced fresh paper towels.

It occurred to me that while I had been quick the year before to launch inquiries into why we couldn't get this right, I had not been so quick to ask the question, "Who is responsible for there *always* being paper towels in the bathrooms these days?" I was slow to recognize that this wasn't happening by accident and that the cause must have been human.

How often do you encounter things that are exactly as you want them to be within your business and ask the question, "Who is responsible for this?"? You may make a point of praising someone for doing a good job if he or she is right in front of you or in response to being presented with something that meets expectations. The real test is how good you are at going out of your way to ask "Who keeps producing these reports that are always timely and accurate?" or "Who keeps this cafeteria so clean and tidy?" "Where can I find the person responsible so I may express my appreciation for their consistent efforts?"

When the CEO of a large company walks down three floors to find and compliment the person who compiles the reports he or she sees every day, the message is loud and clear. These are the standards promoted and expected within the organization and it does not go unnoticed when they are achieved.

As with information, how well you communicate the consequences of something slipping through the net can make all the difference to an employee's ability to understand the problem. The opportunity to go through a full analysis of how the problem has affected your business, and therefore your customers and your employees, is one that should not be wasted.

It's assessment time again. Take a moment to reflect upon your own fuse rating for tolerance. Look around; be honest with yourself about what you see, paying close attention to the telltale signs of a fuse that has too high a rating. Reflect on previous issues you have had with your key personnel. How many after review were related to the individual's overrated tolerance fuse? When recalling instances that you believe should have been taken care of before they got to you, who in your team failed to deal with them? What do you do to foster a culture of low tolerance for things below par in your business? Do you do anything? Could you do more?

Once again, to help with making an assessment in each element, I have listed the things you should look at. Take stock of the results and use them to rate where you currently stand and use the same rating device as before.

Element	Assessment
What is my fuse rating? Think about what you let people get away with and how often you let things slip by. Look at the frequency of employees presenting work to you that they know to be below par.	
What are the ratings of my key personnel? Look at the things that get to you but should have been caught by someone else first. Review how you assess why something unacceptable to you got through other members of your team.	
What mechanisms are currently in place? Think about how good you are at noticing why something goes well and who is responsible.	

Refer back to the end of chapter four. Apply the same approach to assessing and improving the tolerance fuse ratings within your business.

The focus areas for tolerance may be different than those for information. In both cases, start with where the need is greatest.

Chapter 7

COACHING & DISCIPLINE:
The Two-way Approach

When it comes to getting a true sense of someone's fuse ratings for information and tolerance, there is no better opportunity than when you are called upon to be the coach or disciplinarian.

The first two things to remember about coaching and discipline are:

1. Coaching can occur without discipline

2. Discipline should never occur without coaching

There are many times when coaching is offered not as correction but as initial training or continued guidance on how to do a job well. This is the execution stage of your business plan and is on the other side of the Consistency Gap.

When it is necessary to be the disciplinarian correcting unacceptable behavior or performance, it is a crime not to include an element of coaching to fix the problem for the future. If your true goal in discipline is to point out to your employees that certain behavior or a certain standard of work is unacceptable and will not be tolerated, you cannot close the discussion without making it clear what *is* acceptable. However, more often than not, this tends to become a one-way street.

Because fixing the problem is always a priority, most instances of corrective discipline involve one-way traffic. When a manager sees an employee doing something in an unacceptable fashion, typically he or she is quick to point this out. A very familiar exchange to most managers would go something like this:

"Joe, I'd like a word with you in private please"

"Yes Ms. Johnson, what can I help you with?"

"Joe, I have just been down to the main lobby to take a look at the work you did today on the display case. I have to say that the quality of the repair was not as I had expected. Specifically, the additional shelving does not appear to be level, the new glass was not cleaned of fingerprints after installation and the lock was not replaced."

"I'm sorry, Ms. Johnson."

"Joe, I would like you to take care of the items I've just mentioned and also learn from this conversation. I will not tolerate work of this standard in the future. Everything we do here must have the appearance of professionalism and accuracy and your job site must always be left clean, tidy, and safe upon completion."

"Again, I'm sorry, Ms. Johnson, I'll take care of it immediately and it won't happen again."

One-way street

You may say that this was a pretty good exchange between the employee and his supervisor. It touched upon all the relevant points, conveyed the reasons for dissatisfaction and set the threshold for future work. All true, but the interaction is entirely one way. What did Ms. Johnson learn about Joe's fuse ratings in this exchange? What was learned about the reasons behind the substandard performance on this particular job? While it can be categorized as somewhat disciplinary, there was very little coaching and absolutely no opportunity taken to learn why the problem occurred in the first place. Furthermore, you can only move on to coaching about how fuse ratings can be improved after having assessed them.

When encountering substandard performance, take the time to work through a process. The first thing you should want to know when something has tripped your tolerance fuse is why it didn't trip the fuse of the person responsible. Instead of immediately explaining that you are not satisfied, first ask if *they* find the work satisfactory. The final outcome on the display case job may or may not have been satisfactory to Joe, but do not begin addressing the problem by assuming you know which it is. Wouldn't you want to know whether Joe actually thought the job looked good enough? It is not enough to say that he must have thought so or he wouldn't have left it that way.

There are a number of things you should want to find out as a result of such an exchange.

"Joe, does this look acceptable to you?"

Standing side by side with Joe in front of the display case, with slanted shelves, greasy fingerprints on the glass and a missing lock, what are Joe's choices when he is asked this question? It is not a trap, nor a clever ploy that leaves Joe no good way out. It should be expressed as a genuine effort to find out whether Joe feels that the job looks okay. Only after determining this, can you move forward with the coaching.

"It looks okay to me, Ms. Johnson."

A quick check is necessary here just to settle your mind that Joe is not just defending his position and that he really does not see anything wrong with the standard of work, after which, you will have determined that Joe's fuse rating for tolerance of substandard work is way too high. Once this has been established, the next steps include demonstration of the problem, training, re-assignment or replacement.

Take the time to go through the problems, highlighting the consequences of the specific shortcomings of the job. Ask Joe to verbally paint the picture for a good-looking display case. Once he has done so, point out that his description did not include slanted shelves and greasy fingerprints. Explain the impact that the loss of the display case contents would have on the company due to the absence of the lock. Make arrangements to place Joe with another more trusted worker for more structured training. If necessary, re-assign him to other duties within his skill base or ultimately, replace him.

"Actually, no – it does not look okay to me"

This is where it gets interesting. If it was not acceptable, then why did he leave the job that way? If he wasn't happy with it, why wasn't his fuse tripped, leaving him compelled to go back and take another shot at it? These are the things you must find out in order to truly determine the problem. Answers can be widely varied and often relate to some other pressure being experienced by Joe that trumped his personal values and standards. If you have a good employee in Joe, this shouldn't happen very easily, and the pressure must be pretty severe. You need to uncover the forces at work strong enough to override his standards of performance.

They can include lack of time, lack of equipment/tools/resources, lack of direction, or just over-tasking. They can also include non-work related pressures. In any event, without taking the time to get to this stage, you will likely fix the immediate problem but do nothing to address the root cause, thus walking away from the situation having learned nothing and leaving Joe with exactly the same fuse rating as when you found him.

The above process can quickly lead you into "information" territory. If you have established that Joe was conflicted in how the job was finished and he did have compelling reasons for selling his own standards short, you can assume he didn't get that way overnight. How did this situation evolve without you knowing about it? Why wasn't Joe's first thought to go to someone and explain that the pressures he was experiencing were preventing him from doing his job well?

These are questions you must ask. No one is going to ask them for you. In most cases this is the only way of taking full advantage of one of the best ways to assess the fuse ratings of the people you employ.

Assessing the information fuse of everyone in the team using a coaching approach is somewhat easier. When something didn't get through that should have, it is usually easy to trace it back through the line to the point where a fuse tripped and the progress stopped. Many times this can be at the actual source of the information and the rest of the circuit doesn't even come into play.

For example, how many times have you generated information that is useful to a number of players on your team and simply missed one person or one department from the copy list? You typically find this out when the same person or department winds up doing something they shouldn't because they didn't know things had changed. It's an easy error and is made both at the beginning of the line and at any point in the line on an everyday basis.

When this happens however, what do you do to find out why the information was not adequately disseminated? Was it simple error - someone just forgetting to include marketing or legal on the memo? Was it a lack of understanding on the importance or value of the data? Or was it just bad judgment on who should and should not be informed?

All these questions need to be answered before you can apply the appropriate technique to fix the fuse in question. As previously mentioned, it may just be the absence of an information-sharing culture in your organization.

Some imagery that has proven useful to me over the years is to relate information to medicine. As the one in possession of information, you hold medicine that can be critical to others. It can come in two forms:

1. Treatment

2. Inoculation

Treatment with the Information medicine is given in order to assist those who are already in need of it so they may deal with a specific issue that has arisen. *"Cut the blue wire now"* springs to mind.

Inoculation with the Information medicine is a proactive approach to hopefully avert the occurrence of the issue in the first place. *"Failure to wear the proper safety restraints may result in injury or death"*

Whenever I have information in hand, I try to first categorize it as treatment or inoculation and then decide who needs it. Sometimes the same piece of information is inoculation to some people and treatment to others. It is always worth thinking for a moment that if someone needed to be treated with a particular medicine, it probably makes sense to inoculate others as a precaution.

No matter how the information is characterized, the imagery of medicine just helps to remind me how critical it can be to get it out to those who need it, and to do so quickly. It also prompts me to think through the chain: who could possibly need this or would benefit from it in any way?

I have also found that the analogy holds true in another way. The more thorough you become with your inoculations, the less treatment you need to administer down the road.

Find a tool that works for you, one that helps you coach those with a weak information fuse so that they understand what is needed to increase their fuse rating in this area. Finally, test for the presence and vibrancy of the culture every day. Check for conflicting messages and look for signs that the crowd seems to be marching to the beat of a drum different to the one *you* think you are playing.

I have always believed that I have successfully communicated my values on information sharing. I believe that those who have worked with and for me really do understand that my information fuse is really hard to trip.

A number of years ago, a member of my staff was looking for a suitable birthday gift for me and decided to show me the gift in a catalogue first because she was not sure if I would appreciate it - or even find it funny.

The proposed gift was a rustic wooden sign for outside my office that said:

Nobody Gets In
To See The Wizard,
Not Nobody,
Not No How!

My first reaction was similar to what was going through the mind of my team member. I won't be able to display this because it's not true; therefore, she was somewhat surprised when I said I would like it as a birthday gift.

When the sign arrived, it was installed immediately. People commented on the sign, sometimes just seeing it as an amusing decoration, but often asking why I had it on the wall when no one seemed to pay any attention to it.

Well, there it is. The real test of my own information sharing culture theory was to post a sign that is completely contrary to what I practice and see what happens.

The sign was completely ignored!

Those who work with me know that they can bring information to me any time they like. They are sure of this as a result of my behavior and not what the sign says.

Chapter 8

THE THREE ELEMENTS: The 30/50/20 Rule

At the outset, I belabored the point that only two things are responsible for the Consistency Gap. I have repeatedly made the argument that all things, which go uncorrected within your business, are the result of:

An inability or reluctance to handle large volumes of information.

Or;

A tendency to accept poor quality or performance.

Or;

Both.

No matter what sub-standard conditions might currently exist in your business, you cannot avoid the fact that they exist either because you didn't know about them or because you have been tolerating them up to this point.

The good news is that because only two things are responsible, correction is a relatively focused task and will have a huge effect on your business.

Eventually however, you may discover or create a *third* element to the Consistency Gap:

1. Things you didn't know about.

2. Things you were tolerating unnecessarily.

3. *Things you had elected to tolerate for good reason.*

In general terms, I believe that these three elements are responsible for all unchecked shortfalls and failures in any business, in the following proportions:

About 30% of the things that do not meet the standard are there because you didn't know about them, things that are going on that never get to you and therefore deprive you of any opportunity to prevent or fix them.

About 50% are there because they are being unnecessarily tolerated, either consciously or sub-consciously. These are the things that could be fixed if you made the decision to fix them. That is not to say that these are the things which are easy to fix or that could be fixed quickly. You may not even relish the thought of fixing them. The point is they could be fixed if you set your mind to the task.

What's stopping me?

A simple test when finally noticing or becoming aware of the things that fall into this 50% grouping is to stop and ask: "What is stopping me from fixing that?"

You will find that it isn't always because it would cost too much money or require resources you don't have. You will just as often find that other than the time and commitment involved, nothing has been stopping you from fixing it.

The remaining 20% are there because, after full deliberation, you have determined that you have no choice. The costs, resources, and implications involved simply mean that it cannot be fixed. Be careful with the word "*cannot*" however. This should only apply when the consequences of correction are more damaging to your business than the benefits of the correction itself. In such cases, I tend to change the language a little to put these items in perspective. I regard them as things which, when all things are considered, *"should not"* be fixed.

You will know when you have this right. The only items that continue to go uncorrected in your business are not items that can't be fixed. They are items that, on balance, shouldn't be fixed.

Under this 30/50/20 Rule, it is plain to see that a full 80% of what tends to go uncorrected in your business is within your control and can be fixed.

Fractions of fractions

Don't get hung up on the remaining 20%. Suppose for a moment that as much as 5% of your product or service fails to meet the standard you have set for your business. 20% or one fifth of that 5% left uncorrected means that only 1% of your product or service will be running below par by choice, leaving you with a 99% success rate in achieving your own standards.

Conclusion

If you are to fully embrace and benefit from this approach to bridging or eliminating the gap between planning and execution, you are called upon to do several things.

1. You must first come to terms with the fact that there *is* a gap between the plan and the day-to-day execution of the plan. Any frustration you have felt over not getting it right every time can be attributable to not being aware of the existence of this gap.

2. You must put your excuses to the test. Do they stand up to the "only two things" concept? Once you are able to accept that uncorrected problems exist either because you did not know about them or because you were tolerating them, you are well on the way.

3. You must understand that the people who work for you take their lead from the culture you foster and enforce, not from paper policy.

4. You must take the time to assess your own fuse ratings and the ratings of those who work for you.

5. You must create or improve upon a culture within your business that promotes information sharing and zero tolerance for anything below par.

6. Your goal is to begin raising your own information fuse rating as high as you can stand it, and then use the tools in this book to raise the ratings of your team. You also need to lower your tolerance fuse rating to the point where it is tripped by the smallest of things. This alone will force the rest of your team to do the same.

The imagery pictured back in Chapter Two does not truly symbolize where you and your team need to be. When applying the principles in this book to your business on a daily basis, the following imagery better depicts where you and your team will be.

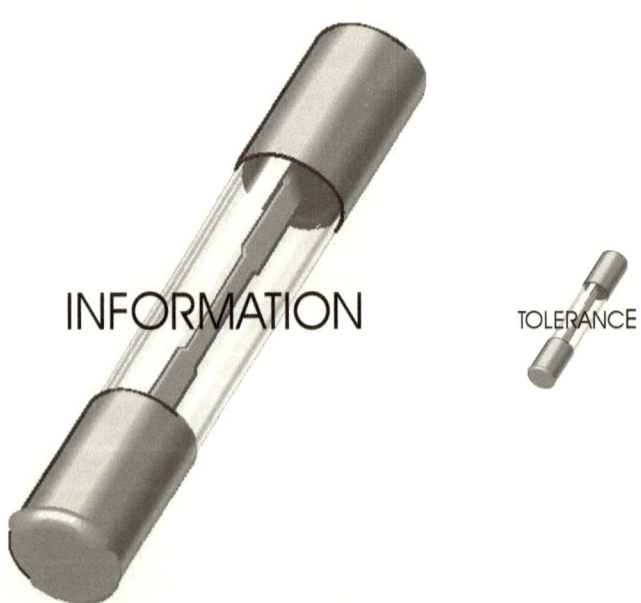

Use of this imagery can be fun. Application of the principles it symbolizes can help set and explain the priorities for any employee at any level with every type of responsibility.

The results can be spectacular.

Appendix A

The general purpose of a fuse in an electrical circuit is to limit the flow of current passing through it. In instances where the current is very heavy, the fuse needs to be large in order to handle the flow and where the current is very low, the fuse is typically very small.

In all cases, the fuse is designed to handle a certain maximum current which, when exceeded, will essentially melt a metal link within the fuse and interrupt the flow of current passing through it. As such, a fuse is designed to manage and in particular, limit the flow of current through a circuit to prevent damage further down the line.

In general terms, if you want a lot of current to get through, the fuse needs to be very large to cope with it, but if you want to limit the current getting through to very low levels, the fuse needs to be so small and sensitive that it will blow very quickly.

With these properties in mind, turn back to page 5 and you will begin to visualize how they apply to the two key elements that cause the Consistency Gap.

About the Author:

Over the past 25 years, Mark S. Turner has written and presented training material tailored specifically to the hospitality industry. He has spoken at International Conventions including the International Association of Amusement Parks & Attractions (IAAPA) and the National Association of RV Parks and Campgrounds (ARVC). He has also participated as a faculty member in the Graduate Program at the National School of Resort Management based at the Oglebay Resort in Wheeling, West Virginia.

He was Vice President of the British and American Chamber of Commerce for Central Florida in 1994 and 1995 and was a member of the Board of Directors of (ARVC) from 2002 to 2006, serving as Chairman of their National Governance Committee and as National Treasurer.

Mark has been involved in the general management of businesses in the hotel and leisure resort industry for more than 30 years in Europe and the United States. He became involved in the European resort industry in the 1970s, holding management and product development positions with companies including Grand Metropolitan Hotels, Guinness Leisure Holdings, Haven Holidays and the Rank Group, PLC. Mark moved to the United States in the mid 1990s and continues to be involved in resort and real estate ownership, management and development in Pennsylvania.

Index

U

Unchecked, 9

V

Verbal cues, 31
Visual cues, 31

W

What's stopping me?, 82
Word of mouth, 31

Y

Your own fuse ratings, 3, 18, 85
Your key personnel, 19, 33, 40, 59, 66